THE URBAN
STAMPEDE

THE URBAN STAMPEDE

and Other Poems

F.D. Reeve

Michigan State University Press
East Lansing

⊗ The paper used in this publication meets the mini-
mum requirements of ANSI/NISO Z39.48–1992
(R 1997) (Permanence of Paper).

Michigan State University Press
East Lansing, Michigan 48823-5202

Printed and bound in the United States of America.

07 06 05 04 03 02 01 1 2 3 4 5 6 7 8 9 10

LIBRARY OF CONGRESS CATALOGING-IN-
PUBLICATION DATA

Reeve, F.D. (Franklin D.), 1928–
The urban stampede and other poems / F.D. Reeve.
    p. cm.
ISBN 0-87013-594-5 (pbk. : alk. paper)
1. Orpheus (Greek mythology) — Poetry.
2. Eurydice (Greek mythology) — Poetry.   I. Title.
PS3568.E44 U73 2001
811'.54 — DC21

                                    2001002839

Grateful acknowledgment is made to the editors of
the following magazines in which these poems previ-
ously appeared: *AGNI, The Connecticut Review,
The Hudson Review, The New Criterion, The North
Dakota Quarterly, Poetry, a Magazine of Verse,
The Sewanee Review* and *The Southwest Review.*

"On October Ground" illustrated Thomas L. Read's
orchestral suite for the Vermont Symphony Orchestra,
autumn 1998.

"The Urban Stampede," a chamber oratorio with
music by Andrew Gant, received its world premiere
at St. Giles Cripplegate, The Barbican, London, on
14 April 2000.

Book design by Valerie Brewster, Scribe Typography
Cover Artwork is used courtesy of the artist,
Lawrence F. Holbrook.

Visit Michigan State University Press on the World
Wide Web at:

www.msupress.msu.edu

for Jay and Martha

Io mi volsi di retro allora tutto
a' miei poeti, e vidi che con riso
udito avevan l' ultimo construtto;

poi alla bella donna tornai il viso.

Contents

THE URBAN
STAMPEDE

THE URBAN
STAMPEDE

Proem

The action takes place in a large city in the People's Bar, known as *The Urban Stampede*. Everyone is there, warts and all. No one, except the bartender and the waiters, has any useful work to do. Things happen one after another, as if time were passing, but nothing changes.

A few extraordinary customers are in a state of perpetual penance for having grossly exceeded proper claims in the world outside the bar.

Figures in the Bar

THE CHORUS

Young men and women waiting tables in The Urban Stampede;

Harry Hayden — every inch the bartender of The Urban Stampede;

Theobald — a wealthy but unscrupulous political adviser who has sold about as many secrets as he ever learned;

Novello — a movie star, a matinee idol, gorgeous and stupid;

Sheffield — an *ex-mafioso* who, after moving into the plumbing and heating business, never went straight;

Edelmar — owner of a huge paper manufacturing company, a man who clear-cut whole townships;

Thorley — a great local hero and retired general whose power went to his head; with Pomeroy he tried to kidnap his company president's wife;

Pomeroy — the world's richest computer magnate who tried to make virtual reality come true;

Parnella — Harry Hayden's beautiful wife.

MACK

a handsome young man, a great singer and guitarist. He looks for Mary May, finds her in the bar, and persuades her to come home.

5

As they're about to leave, they get their signals crossed—Mack isn't aware she's deaf—and she again disappears.

MARY MAY
a gorgeous young woman, Mack's wife, who became seriously deranged from illness and disappeared. Lost and lonely, she wanders through the bar hearing nothing, unaware that the illness has made her deaf.

Another Figure

BORN OBSERVER
a cool cat whose recitative keeps things moving along.

The Urban Stampede

CHORUS
 Here in the Urban Stampede
 the beer's the best value in town;
 the drinks are the cheapest in all of (*city of present
   performance*),
 and the coffee is richer and sweeter
 than any place else you might treat her;
 so, do yourselves, boys, a favor:
 buy two regular flavors,
 and we'll brew you a third for free.

BORN OBSERVER
 The white porch rose beyond the elms
 where in the crowns cardinals in March
 sang their pure notes as if the sap
 were running up their legs and out
 their throats. To the right there was a high
 brick terrace overlooking the pond
 with its bathhouse, dock and little boat,
 the cedar skiff her father made
 by bending well-steamed planks across
 a mold, then fiberglassing over.
 Round and round in that little craft
 went Mary May and Mack, her lover,
 he plying the oars as if plucking a lyre,
 she trailing her hand through the soft water
 past lily pads and fat sleepy carp.
 Summer: the scent of new-mown hay;
 the sun warm on their brown skins,
 by night the thunder of desire,
 by morning the angle of repose.

CHORUS
  Here in the Urban Stampede
  you get only the cream of the crop:
  the clientele are divine;
  the cooks are immortal;
  the barman's a saint;
  the waiters are angels;
  and the menus are tops.

MACK
  O dancer, o world that turns in sunlight!
  whose hand sweeps the air like a bird!
  who rises on the spindle of desire
  like a velvet flower in a dream!
  You lift; you pirouette — the dark
  recedes — your fingertips leave trails
  of ecstasy along the sky;
  your feet cast shadows on the morning dew.
  At the still center of the turning earth
  your vase of loveliness turns still.

BORN OBSERVER
  When Mary May and Mack made love
  she took pure honey from his hands
  and raised it to her lips as if
  he were divine; for him her honeyed
  lips on his, her hands, light on
  his shoulders, then sliding round his neck,
  her languid, lovely body pressed
  the length of his, electrified
  desire; so, when she looked up
  from the honey comb, he smiled and took
  her in his arms, and she, ecstatic,
  like an animal that hears a noise
  or sees a shadow or smells strange scent,
  startled, froze, then felt the familiar,

and welcoming the burly shoulders,
the patient, firm, sweet-musicked hands,
softened in the warmth like golden honey.

MACK

O come and go. You, my love, gather
minutes like cornflowers from a field,
turn with the trees in arabesques of weather.
Red rose of my imagination, shield

me against the brazen disorderings of nature,
the flaws of love, the sloughs and wastes of time.
I hear your feet roused by my music's figure
tapping their constellations across the sky.

I see you on point drawing to the well,
apple blossoms in your hair, the tree bent low,
you reaching for my shimmering guitar.

Come to me. The birds sing like bells
as you pirouette through the gloaming, bow to applause,
arms spread wide, and open up your heart.

MARY MAY

If I were a mountain stream
tumbling down the granite hills,
I'd play substantial parts in dreams,
not say 'Perhaps' but 'You bet I will.'
I'd carry news of life's success
to homeless people in every town,
make sure each poor child was well dressed,
and in thunderstorms, like an artist stand
facing the wind with open arms.
If I were a mountain stream
I'd make a music all my own;
I'd still awaken with the bees

gathering their morning honey,
smell the rose and the resinous pine
and the honeysuckle on the elderberry . . .

CHORUS
Here in the Urban Stampede
we've got everything you need
for a perfect evening out:
If you ain't got much money
you can still treat your honey
to a glass of Lauderdale stout
or recite her some *Hamlet*
while we fry you an omelette
and figure the charges out.

BORN OBSERVER
What a wedding it was — two perfect people:
with a swaying, liquid grace
her passing stirred the summer leaves;
the flowers nodded where he stood;
the birds then crowded to him. Strangers
claimed him as their long-lost son.
He's so yare, the old men said,
he sits a horse like a fairy king.
So, when the lovers stood beneath the canopy
of elm and willow at the pond
the clouds applauded in pure delight.
He held her a long time in his arms;
she then drew his head down to her breast
like two goldfinches in the sun.
Then slowly, strangely, she lost her way
among small assignments. Then the shape
and purposes of life withdrew,
and she herself said 'Shelved,' 'remaindered.'
Everything was turning gray.
The pond had gone. She lived in twilight.

And he—he sounded so far away.
Had he really loved her once?
She remembered how his hands had held
her shoulders the first time that he kissed her,
and she reached out for his hands. "Mack!"
No shadow lay upon the ground,
no shade of love, as if the elms
had dropped their leaves and the willows wept
because the world was no longer fair.

CHORUS
No need to go to school
to play it cool; don't be a fool;
you make your own rules.
The first one, like in thermodynamics,
or pottery when you break some ceramics,
says you keep all the pieces.
Like having nephews and nieces,
or crying and laughter,
you've always got the same before and after.
Doesn't matter who they choose,
that way you never lose.
All the garbage they throw at us! Don't be a sap;
recognize it as the crap
it is. You want red meat or you want tripe?
Believe us, man; don't believe the hype!
If the love of your life went off on her own,
what would you do? Wouldn't you head
for the nearest bar? Death calls for a drink.
Madame Ouijanovsky casts the cards
that promise the soul's immortality.
Two for one, Madame Ouijanovsky says,
so, everyone goes to The Urban Stampede
for love and everything else they need—

BORN OBSERVER

Harry Hayden was tending bar,
his wife Parnella washing up,
when Mary May came drifting in.
He was talking to a regular
unaccustomed to the view. What view?
His name was Theobald. He thought
he saw a mountain lake reflected
in the sky, but Harry said it was
a mirror, part of the bar's enchantment,
and asked what kind of drink he'd like.
"When you look in the mirror," Harry said,
"you see who's coming from behind."

CHORUS

Look in the mirror, look in the mirror!
Look who's coming from behind!

BORN OBSERVER

"Scotch and soda," said Theobald,
but as Harry poured, the bottle dried.
"O please, a drink! I'm dying of thirst!"
wailed Theobald as again Harry tried.
"Cut it out!" shouted Harry back;
"all the bottles I pour for you
are empty! That's some trick! You guys—"

CHORUS

Nothing to eat, nothing to drink,
nothing to say and nothing to think—

BORN OBSERVER

Theobald interrupted to complain
the ceiling fan was loose, it might fall.
"I hope it does," said Harry; "I think
if it did it might take your mind off drink."

Then Theo asked if he could have a pear
(there was a bowlful sitting there)
but when Harry pushed it down the bar
it rolled in the opposite direction.
"O bowl, o pears! O why you, too?
O why is everyone against me?"
"I'm not," said Harry, "if that counts;
as for the rest, how would I know?
It don't pay to analyze,
though from time to time you're tantalized."
That's when Mary May came forward
from the shadows where she had been standing.
Her calf had a soft, seductive curve;
her gait, a lift as if she walked on air.
Where was she now? Why all the silence?
What had she become? A breeze?
A cloud? The music in her head?
Bound to the ground like a tall oak tree,
she waved in the wind, longing to be free.
Barefoot in her imagination
she sailed to the bar through the soft summer air
over the pyrogenic hills
past Sheffield screaming at his game—
"Come on, little ball! Roll up, roll round!
Now left! Now right! Out through the gates
past the bump and the grind—oh no!" One down.
The next—pull back—all set—release!
"Come on, little ball! Roll up, roll round!
Now left! Now right! You son of a bitch!"

CHORUS

Come on, little ball! Roll up, roll round!
Now left! Now right! Out through the gates
past the bump and the grind—oh no! One down.
The next—pull back—all set—release!
Come on, little ball! Roll up, roll round!

BORN OBSERVER

It's only a game. No money involved.
Screw that. No point if you never win.
Or some bastard's always tilting the table.
Leave it? No way. "How can I leave it?
I love it," he said. Pull the plunger again.
"Who are you?" he asked Mary May.
"You act crazy like Charlotte Corday
or Ophelia. Don't worry, sweetheart," he said,
"I won't hurt you. I've got twenty minutes
while the Old Boy untilts the table
before I start in again. What're you drinking?"

CHORUS

For now sit back, drink up. We'll sing
a little anti-revolutionary ditty,
because there's no way here in your favorite city
the management will ever change.
No reason to. It's all well run.
A beer? Some wine? A world-wide range,
plus games of chance and games for fun —
for special customers like you
we have our own dark microbrew.

BORN OBSERVER

The soul is a mirage that drifts on the wind,
a thingless shadow shunting back and forth
through an eternal twilight. The evening star
rises ever more brightly as the sun goes down.

Is she or isn't she? No one says a word.
In the deep silence of the bar not a bird.
Before dawn breaks there's nothing really there
save a faint sky reflecting her silver hair.

"Oh, beautiful!" the young men say,
but what's *beautiful* today?
Mary May is passionate and sad;
poor Mack wants the love he had.
And there sits Novello on his ass
staring into an empty glass.
The face he sees he thinks his own
though nothing's there but silicon.
When he holds up a glass to see
what nature is, it's himself he sees.
When nature picks the best it's done,
it tells him he's the only one.
All the praise of birds and bees
won't explain the spring's new leaves.
When a new queen comes along
a hive of bees will split and swarm.
A man in love whose lips are pressed
to his true love's sweet-flowing breast —
it's much too hackneyed; the moral, hard;
but think — 'Heloise and Abelard.'
A dark-eyed demoiselle's blonde head
enchants with sadness, but instead
of leading men to glorious death
(Cleopatra comes to mind,
who as a lover was not unkind)
it simply takes away their breath.
So after Harry draws her beer
he calls out to the rest, "Wait, boys,
I'm coming! This here gent was first."
Old Edelmar, the clear-cut man,
a glutton and schlimazel, called for
three ham sandwiches, a dozen brews,
two plates of fries, one chef's salad
and an apple pie. "You and who else,"
says Harry. "Me, myself and I,"
Edelmar replies and downs

the ketchup bottle and the sugar.
Harry's knees now knock like doorknobs:
"Good god, the glassware and the china!
I'll get your order right away!"
He goes out; the fat man starts in:
"Listen, all of you! The world, my friends,
was made for us and is to be
consumed. To be here is to be rich.
He who eats an oyster on
St. James's Day will never want.
What are trees but natural food?
The rocks, our natural furniture?
Beneath this round earth's soil and seas
there lies a store of liquid gold.
Every green and growing thing,
every thing that creeps or crawls,
or flies or swims or by some chance
lands on our land, belongs to us.
Aha! My lunch!" Harry says,
"I'll set some over here. Can you reach?
There's no room along the bar."
"There's room for me," says Edelmar,
"and that's enough. Pass me that plate!
Make way for my stomach! More lunch!
I'm so good at eating, see,
I could even eat myself."
His lucubrations were cut short
by twin simultaneous arrivals:
a tray of bouillabasse and bread,
paiella, penne, pork crown—and Mack.

CHORUS
Stranger, stranger, who are you?
Stranger, stranger, what do you do?
Have you come looking for Mary May?
She's one of us; she's here to stay.

You going to try to take her away?
Harry's the only one can say
        it's okay.
She's not well, see, not today—
        no way.

MACK

When I remember how she charmed the night,
the campfire blazing, a chill air off the lake,
from far away the late-summer cry of a loon,
I see the raptured faces of first love,
a semi-circle of dark, sparkling eyes,
and hands begging more songs of pure delight.

I watch our shadows dancing while we sit.
Tall tamaracks bend low; the wind rises.
Are the deer, the fox, the bear, the toads, the birds
that keep the woods bending an ear behind
the illuminated circle? In their wild patience
do they sense a second coming? Is this music of it?

Ambition swarms, but creative work remains
all delicate flowers. The songs that like a carpet
lead into life express the oldest news:
The greatest joy is love; the greatest sadness,
to recollect the ecstasy of love
not only lost but lost in endless pain.

CHORUS

Want a toke?
Snort some coke?
The old joint's gone to Hell!
Hell is here
with you, my dear—
we're king and queen as well.
Come up, boys!

Get your joys,
girls, grabbing on their knobs.
Try the test
which sex is best
at grilling shish kabob.
Don't worry, honey,
it's only money
goes down the drain of life.
We have free will
to clip the till
and plow our neighbor's wife.
Look! Here's a couple
who caused trouble
when they kidnapped the boss's gripe.

BORN OBSERVER

All the waiters in the bar
dislike both Pomeroy and Thorley,
who used the power of the state
to line their pockets and get their enemies
(much like Bill and the Watergates).
Half the day and half the night
they argue over who is right
about things long gone, things they'll never do,
things I'd not think of — nor would you.
Says Thorley first, "Here's the poop,
which I got from A.D. Hope:
the future's a furry, two-inch slit
and everything comes out of it.
Even if she don't want to leave,
that chick's ready for a man to reeve
a hunk of rope right through her block."
Then Pomeroy says, while he scratches his cock,
"If what she wants is a first-rate lay,
there's no reason she'd betray—"
Thorley butts in: "You and TV!

How can you make a real love scene
unless you take your eyes off that fucking screen?"
"I'll start when she comes for the monthly dues."
"When you're done, I'll show how real men screw."
"When I'm done, there'll be nothing left to do.
The women I make make the evening news."
Then Thorley leaves and Pomeroy shouts
as he waves his two hands in the air,
"Pickers-and-stealers, ten fanny feelers!"
And Thorley gives him the finger, of course.

CHORUS

Pickers-and-stealers, ten fanny-feelers!
And Thorley gives him the finger, of course.

BORN OBSERVER

How shall I explain
a king who will not dance?
Of course the world's unfair.
Our lives are shaped by chance.
Consider how snails evolved.
Think of those who've killed
their fathers in fits of anger
for not yielding to their wills.
Of all the people born
who knows who's cursed?
Avoiding a bad death
men often end still worse.
I mourn deductible losses.
I grieve the brave talents
vanished like dreams, drugged,
wasted by accidents,
their purposes undone,
circling among the dark
stars like angels, alone,
waiting to come back

to earth in different bodies,
Fate swings coldly out of Limbo
like the winter wind through the windows
to draw the warmth from a house.
Pomeroy tried to fly high
but didn't make it. His girlfriend
still says, "What the heck!
At least when he fell he didn't
break his neck."

MARY MAY

    I wander like a shadow
     now that my love's gone;
    I wander like a begging man
    without a home —

MACK

    Somewhere over the world my love walks
       hand in hand with my dreams.
    Somewhere over the world my love talks
       with angels across a heavenly stream.
          O I wish I were there with my love,
            her hand in mine;
          I'd brush the loose hair from her brow
            as true love's sign.

MARY MAY

    Down empty corridors
       and vacant halls

    past crowded rooms
       and mirror-covered walls —

MACK

    How can she be gone
       who had no place to go?

I'll look until the world,
    like the sun, burns out.

CHORUS

Appearances may be deceiving;
the customers are whimsical.
You yourself may easily mistake
an itinerant accordionist for a lover
because, of all the pleasures in the world,
music's the greatest next to love.
Good lovers' stories are make-believe,
but some, like real-life tales, are true.
Of course, the most wonderful of all
are the ones that happened to you.
Here at the Urban Stampede the drinks
get bigger and better the longer you stay,
and everyone drinks and says what she thinks,
and all life's problems go quickly away.

MACK

On Tuesday last my lover and I
spent the whole night in the woods,
playing together, side by side,
till the nightingale sang, as loud as it could,
"Sweet friends, the dawn! It's time to go."
I held her close as I replied,
"O love of my heart, sweet body's delight,
it's not dawn yet, the nightingale lies."
She kissed me back, and so then I
kissed her deeply in those woods;
We wished it would last a hundred nights,
but the nightingale sang, as loud as it could,
"Sweet friends, it's dawn! It's time to go."
She kissed farewell and said with a sigh,
"O love of my heart, sweet body's delight,
it's not dawn yet; the nightingale lies."

CHORUS

Where are you going, handsome young man?
Sit down with us. Let us shake your hand.
Here's a cushion. Together we'll watch the screen
for everything that will be and has been.
Everything happens here in full view:
you see into us, and we see into you.

MACK

Can you tell me where she's hiding,
          Harry-O?
Can you tell me who's a-loving,
          Harry-O?
Have you got the latest tidings,
          Harry-O?

Eating's said to prove a pudding,
but seeing's all we need for loving,
          Harry-O!

MARY MAY

Blue into blue into blue
    the water runs into the hills,
the rocks and firs stand still,
    and the clouds roll on and on.

The wind from the West blows warm
    across meadowsweet, briar rose
and the osprey circling the cove
    where white boats come and go.

Sun holding the sky like a keystone,
    sea cupped in the palm of your hand—
the paradise of Cockaigne
    and you under sail toward it,
    and the wind never changing again.

MACK

I hear you, baby; I got you now,
here comes a shot cross your bow
        with love.
I was lying low, I was going slow,
I didn't know what I had to show
        but love.
The city dames — don't know their names —
all the same I played their game
        of love.
Hey, where you hiding, I'm going riding,
no more uptight, I'm out tonight
        for love.
You got it, I want it,
you want it, I got it,
I'm coming,
        that's love.

CHORUS

O you two lovers, are you so there you're already over?
Like, if you're fixing on becoming barroom rovers
you've got to make up songs that tell the facts,
because life's conditions change. Like, white ain't black.
And if you think yourselves so smart, while you're able
you better switch from the networks back to cable.
Small is beautiful: believe us when we say
the less you do, the more you get your way.
Now for Edelmar and Parnella, too,
here's a song to put them in the mood:
Life is music; music, life.
I love my food; my food's my wife.
I take a thousand wives to bed —
sugarplums dancing in my head —
and when I wake, a thousand more
stand waiting for me at the door.
One thousand one, one thousand two,

I do the thing I have to do.
Life is music; music, life.
I love my food; my food's my wife.

BORN OBSERVER

O ye people of little faith,
what shall we do for allegory?
In these saurian times, when men and women
without a nickel to their names
imagine camping trips to Paradise,
how can we know who's a stranger, who belongs?
The frightening fact that still is true
is that people won't accept your views
until everyone else is through with you.
Even lovers find they have to go,
like Juliet and her Romeo,
in order for their love to last.

MACK

Sing, sweet voices in my head,
the story of two gentle lovers,
each the other's lodestar, lost
in the teeming bar, who searched for the future
in the shadows and the rough, dark waste
of the past hunting a fragment of news,
a shoe, an envelope, a strand of hair,
a chance remark the barman heard.
Remind me how unfairly it
began, what haze slowly curtained off
her mind and sent him wildly looking
through the stinking alleys of desire
for the lady who had laid her face
in his hands and lain across his heart.
Tell of hours trying to please strangers,
of nights trying to sleep through cold rain,
of moments of almost meeting when,

like the doors snapping shut on a subway train,
everything was cut off, and the future
sped into the dark around the earth.
Say how his heart rose and fell
on the sea that surrounds it, how the fish
heaved with hope, arose from despair —
embellish, exaggerate, refine,
perpetrate the illusions of madness,
people the imagined truth.
Eyelashes, ounces, weeds' Latin names —
everything sings. All the songs
make up the music of the spheres —
for this is my story, and the story of my love:
my love is blonde with coal-black hair;
she has two brown blue eyes;
her heart and mine make up a pair;
we're as tall as our arms are wide.
I'm coming, love; here I come.

CHORUS
Mary May and Mack haven't rebegun;
Harry and Parnella are damned near done;
so, here's a little ballad we've made up
to help all lovers pass the loving cup:
A travelling man came into a bar,
        hi-de-ho,
"Give me a double, I'm riding far,"
        hi-de-ho.
The bartender said as he passed him his drink,
"Ain't your face familiar? I think
you was down on the post office wall
accused of killing John J. Ball."
As he downed his scotch the man replied,
        hi-de-ho,
"I'll tell you the truth, John Ball — he lied,"
        hi-de-ho,

"he cheated the people and stole from the state,
embezzled from widows and swiped church plate;
now he's doing his thing as a rolling head,
an underworld football for the dead."
"From your story I see you're a man of parts
and surely know all the musical arts.
Drinks on the house—that's for a start—
if you can warm my wife's cold heart."
"O la," cried the man, "that's easy to do";
      hi-de-ho,
"a night on the town, a night up and down"
      hi-de-ho,
"tomorrow night she'll be back loving you,"
      hi-de-ho,
"tomorrow night she'll be back loving you."
(*Women's voices*) So what did Harry say, big boy?
(*Men's voices*) Some guys, you know, will rob you blind
   but Harry is the giving kind.
(*Women*) Don't tell me he gave you the shirt off his back.
(*Men*) You do your job well, and so does he.
   This bar's the best that a bar can be.
   The bartender's never on scholarship,
   and the lady-in-charge is really hip.
(*Women*) I like you, too, big boy. You've got
   a very cute face. I bet you'd look hot
   with a ring in each ear and maybe an Earl—
(*Men*) If I were a grain of sand,
   I'd want to make a pearl
   so I could lie upon your neck
   and travel round the world.
(*Women*) You've got some voice, big boy. Me and you
   had better see what we can do.
(*All again*) The man and lady we're waiting for
   are upstairs behind the door
   in the room where Harry fluffs and folds
   the campers that he has to scold.

Meanwhile why not step up here
and we'll bring you a draft real beer?
A good head it has — like Albert E —
the best-brewed beer that beer can be!

MACK

Where do the clouds go when they go across the sky?
Are the trees still there when I close my eyes?
Everything that is is not the thing it seems.
The world awake is sleeping: life is a dream.

How high do flying fish fly? How deep does a whale dive?
What do bees say to each other as they go in and out of the
    hive?
What comes on the flooding tide goes out on the ebbing
    stream.
We sleep to wake; in waking, sleep: life is a dream.

Guinevere loved Lancelot; Juliet, Romeo;
how to write the story every woman knows.
Here and in the hereafter love's the cream of the cream:
coming and going, our days are like grass· life is a dream.

MARY MAY

They say the redness of the rose
        is blood to whet a young man's fancy.
What then of the lamb on the cross?
        Who at daybreak answers the pansy?

The song I sing is not my own.
        My heart was a sheep that went astray.
Thunder and lightning filled my room
        at night, and sunset began my day.

But now my love is here. His face
        shines like a mirror in the dark.

His lips are moving—I miss the words—
      he's come to repossess my heart.

My love, I fly into your arms
      to hold and be held from the lonely night;
In my mind I hear your music charm
      the mountains and lift the morning light.

MACK

How memory turns our lives around!
We change from day to day
as if our heads roamed far
from where our bodies stay,
and like a shell without a snail
we look to the lie
then go where it lay.
My love, my Mary May, shall we dance?
We'll sing and dance down to the bar—
then see if Harry'll let us out the door.

MARY MAY

I think you're talking, but I'm not sure.
Your lips shape words – your gentle lips
that make the songs—now soundless words,
like the signs of fairy rings in dew.
I hear music in my head. Mind, the music!
Love, where's the music from?

MACK

Let me hold you a moment before we dance.
Once we turn I don't dare look back
lest pity overwhelm me and I fall.
Promise you won't disappear?

MARY MAY

> Last night I walked on water
> like the moon. Fish kissed my feet.
> I soared past the gods
> into their gold dome.

MACK

> A light air whispers at sunset
> as the white-throated sparrow calls,
> and the glimmering leaves of the birch
> invite us into the dark. Tell me, love,
> because the future must come from the past,
> can't you hear me calling your name?
> Where are the years that we've lost?.

BORN OBSERVER

> Mack turned, as in the woods a tall
> but leaning maple half sawn through
> twists from its crown the length of its bole,
> pinning the saw and neither standing
> on its own nor going down.
> Her hand in his, side by side,
> they took the stairs as if going home.

CHORUS

> Here comes Mister Ma-ma-mack,
> ghee-tar on his ba-ba-back.
> Where you off to, Mister M,
> now you've found your ladyfriend?

BORN OBSERVER

> The bar is crowded. Many are rude.
> Passing remarks are semi-lewd,
> like Novello's, who dismissively said,
> "Let women go; they're just a drag
> whether or not they're on the rag.

Come, look into this lake and see
how lovable you're meant to be!"
Sheffield thought Mack might make
enough points to win a game. He cried,
"You want to go into the plumbing business?
Come pull the plunger—we can settle later.
I got friends in the highest places.
You live with a dish, you'll get to hate her."
"Too truly tempting the apple of love,"
Theobald philosophized,
"the fingered pear, the delights of sin.
Don't bother to take your girl out the door,
and I'll introduce you to those coming in."
Fat Edelmar whistled from where he sat,
"Pears, apples, oranges—real fruit!
A bushel of each—tout de suite—toot, toot!
Stop running away with my honeybun;
a man like you needs more than one."
Thorley said to Pomeroy
and Pomeroy said to Mack,
"Once you get outside
you'll wish you could come back.
If I were you I'd quit
your lonely busking life
and seriously start thinking
how to get a wife.
Anyone's, we mean—
certainly not your own—
provided you have a way
to get into her home.
Or join us, if you are
an enterprising fellow,
the next time that we try
to make off with Parnella."

To leave a party early isn't easy,
which the regulars thought Mack and Mary May
were doing. They took it personally. "Snobs!"
some said loudly enough to be overheard.
"When they're alone and down they come in here,
but once they've met and set each other up
they run out the door, like to a better party.
Harry, lock the door! Don't let them out!"
Others disagreed: "Everyone
is free to come and go; why not these two?"
"Even people who change their minds must not
be kept against their will. Forget it, Harry."
Most people stared, said nothing. Some ignored
them altogether. A handful looked them up
and down as if about to disassemble
their body parts. A candle in a glass
flickered in the center of each table,
reddening the faces all around.
"Just coming in to say hello," said Mack,
"maybe take a vacation now we're back
together." Mack forgot himself, let go
of Mary May to shake well-wishers' hands,
but without looking round took hers again
when by a gentle push she urged him on.
"Look at the stall and his china plate
making off like to mark the head of state!"
cried Pomeroy. "Babes in a jar,
who do you really think you are?"
Wiping tears of laughter from his eyes,
Edelmar leaned back and wagged his elbows wide
as a shag on a rock flaps its wings to dry.
"Oh let them go," Parnella said with a grin,
"it's Harry and me who bring the business in."
"Like hell! It's my business," Sheffield replied;
"think how I'd make out with her at my side."
Mack pretended not to hear

but put one foot on a vacant chair
and laid his guitar across his knee.
Mary May watched him get set,
where his fingers landed between the frets,
and realized it was an old duet
that he had started singing.

MACK AND MARY MAY

The clouds are thick, the clouds are low,
     the water's gray.
Pirates are hiding in the rocks,
     death comes this way.
Their hair is long, their legs are wood,
     they stomp the sky.
They wash the gold out of the moon;
     they fade the stars.
We drink our tea beside the castle
     that once was Mark's
where Tristan and Isolde died.

The pirates listen, then repeat
     each word we say.
In the garden by the fish pond
     Guinevere waits
though Launcelot won't come again
     and Arthur's gone.
Flowers wither before the snow,
     the heart repents.
Love drives all lovers to their deaths,
     then death relents:
we love together but die alone.

BORN OBSERVER

Enchanted by the song, the rhapsody
of melody and the magic of the tone,
people forgot they were in a bar—it seemed

some imaginary place like Coradine
where in the House of Harvest Melody,
whose origins, they say, are lost in time,
the music comes from small revolving globes
that sound like human voices without words
so pure is the song and so fresh the upland air.
Then suddenly, as at a conductor's sign
an orchestra takes up a single note,
everyone began to shout and clap—

CHORUS

Bravo! Bis! The voice of angels!
The sweetest song of saddest thought!
Two nightingales! They broke my heart!
Don't let them go; we'll never hear
the likes of them again. Once more,
oh please, once more. Everyone's
eyes are filled with tears. Once more!
The sweetest song that was ever sung!
Harry, now, if they want to, you've got to let
them go. Surely they sang for more than supper.
A voice like Mack's will calm the beasts in the field,
persuade the lion to bed beside the lamb
and bring the heavenly kingdom down to earth.

BORN OBSERVER

Mack pretended not to hear what they said
but stepped to talk to Harry at the bar,
and Mary May followed where he led.
"Wait a sec," said Sheffield as he played another game;
"everything seems strangely to have changed.
Look: Theobald has a bottle in his hand,
he just took a drink; Novello's looking glass
has vanished, he's chatting warmly with Parnella;
Edelmar's plate has a ham-on-rye,
beside it, a coffee cup of normal size;

let me pull the plunger before Harry and you begin
to talk about who's going out and who's coming in;
come on, little ball! roll up, roll round!
now left! now right! that's it! go to town!
it went in! it went in! I win! I win!"

CHORUS

O magic music that brings our fortunes home,
o magic music that makes the future sweet.
Our appetites are curbed, our faults, relieved,
and for today at least our sufferings eased.
Perhaps the spell will be broken when you leave,
but while you're here we're under your umbrella
of enchantment. May Harry grant you what you want.
Three cheers for music, the key to mysteries!

MACK

Thank you. Thank you. I'd like to say
what a wonderful audience you are.
I'll ask Harry if we can go,
though certainly we'll miss the bar—

BORN OBSERVER

At that point Edelmar
suggested Mack and Mary May
sing the song again
while they asked Harry on their behalf
to send them on their way.

MACK AND MARY MAY

The clouds are thick,
the clouds are low,
the water's gray.
Pirates are hiding
in the rocks,
death comes this way.
Flowers wither
before the snow,
the heart repents.
Love drives all lovers
to their deaths,
then death relents:
we love together
but die alone.

BORN OBSERVER

Novello first, then Thorley, Pomeroy
and all the rest begged Harry let them go:
"They've earned their freedom, done their best,
You've got to let them go."
"Okay," said Harry, "go they may provided
neither one looks at the other to see
how happy they are and happy they will be."
"What if they do?" Parnella asked, "what then?"
"Then back she comes," stern Harry said,
"no questions asked, no second chance for them."
There was much shuffling on the floor,
some murmuring, some complaints, but when
the song came to its end, and everyone was still,
Mack understood what Harry had commanded
and said, "If we're to go together but
to go blindly, as we have loved, we will."

CHORUS

Some things are black; some things are white;
that's true for people, bears and lights.
The beer we brew is brown or yellow,
full-bodied, dark, rich, pale or mellow.
Though you may think this not the time
to fetch a pilsner or a rhyme,
we of the waitstaff hope you know
even after Mack and Mary go
you can get everything you need
at Harry's famous Urban Stampede.
The universe doesn't have a sequel,
but in here everybody's equal:
no last, no first, so first to last
no one denigrates the past.
White is black and black is white,
everybody's wrong is right.

35

No matter what your partner says
you've got to bid your hand.
It doesn't matter how you feel,
this is reality, and
reality's what's real.

BORN OBSERVER

Escorted by the enthusiastic crowd,
Mack headed for the door, Mary May
a pace or two behind, the people praising
the goodness of the world and his kind heart.
How beautiful she was, they said, how each
of them deserved the other, and the music made
their story into living song. Again
and again they cried as they came up to the door,
"Long live Mack and Mary May!"
"Long live Mack and Mary May!"
In confusion as the swinging doors swung wide,
Mack lost her hand and quickly called her name.
"Mary, come! Now's the time to go!
Farewell friends," he called, "thank you, bless you
for all you've done. Mary, Mary, come!"
She, not hearing, made no move but waited
where she was for his next step ahead;
and he, forgetting where she was and why,
turned to check. The hall fell silent
as they started on the now impossible way.

CHORUS (*reprise under Born Observer's continued recitation*)

O magic music that brings our fortunes home,
o magic music that makes the future sweet.
Our appetites are curbed, our faults, relieved,
and for today at least our sufferings eased.
Perhaps the spell will be broken when you leave,
but while you're here we're under your umbrella

of enchantment. May Harry grant you what you want.
Three cheers for music, the key to mysteries!

BORN OBSERVER

As vague and dark as the shadows between the trees
he keeps coming down the impossible wooden road,
his shoulders rolling as if on the open sea;
his clothing flaps in the wind. What's that in his hand?

Whatever he sees high above the hill
drawing him on, as St. Michael's voice led Joan
and a blinding view of Christ turned Saul to Rome,
delivers him fatally from his own free will.

She follows, head low against the wind on the rise;
her hair whips her face; her thin clothing slips from
          her throat—
numb step after step, dumb through the ravening land.

No love makes up for their loss, not even the prize
of new life. The singing fades on the last plucked note.
And nothing breaks the silence of the wind.

BORN OBSERVER

Slowly Mary May went backward,
not understanding why, forlornly
watching the life she had been a part of
drawn away like blue and distant hills.
Darkness swallowed Mack. Her friends—
she had none now. The glass doors closed.
In her head there rose her plaintive song:

MARY MAY

How many happy years there were!
Now like a colored leaf I spin

away the sunny breeze of summer
down, down the autumn wind.

The past has gone like a frosted face
in the warmth that comes from my window sill.
I see the stars' parabolas
and my lover's orbit round the still

center of my heart. I've done
with the thunder-drum of words, more words.
Silence, like the dying sun,
fills my glass world of love.

BORN OBSERVER

Mack at first was thoroughly surprised
as if fate, like mysterious coincidence,
had intervened, turned time itself around;
but then remembering how she had changed
and he had forgot, he blamed himself alone.
No pardon for it; no consolation, too:
Who'd believe him if he tried to go back?
The night was cold, indifferent. His grief was black
and lay ahead like a desert, a waste of shame.

MACK

Three years we loved, and in the fourth
the moon stood still , stole back our light —
my last illusion, like the harmonies
of childhood's half-forgotten songs.

She vanished in the night as if
the time for love had nothing to it.
Did her solitary deafness
dissolve our composite life?

No point gluing porcelain. Hearts
can't be permanently mended.
My fault; I did it: I broke my life.
Listen: hasn't the music ended?

No, I hear something. I hear her singing.
I picture her at her breakfast table,
the sunlight breaking over Magic Mountain,
the hemlocks silver as when she was a child.
She's playing the piano, a prelude as crystal
as a waterfall in thin mountain air.
Does she hear me in her memory,
sense me standing a little apart?
Surely she dreams of the sounds of music
as green leaves assert the life of a tree.
Wherever she is she must be in heavenly light.
If only I could, I'd tell her, Don't forget
after forty days and nights in the ark
the dove, released, flew back
to the sea-torn longings of its heart.

OTHER
POEMS

The Old World

When I was young the earth was a hard blue globe
    with multi-colored countries and British pinks
    standing by a desk as tall as I
    and spun round by my grandfather's wooden fingers.

Slowly working pause and counterpause
    he crossed deserts, jungles and three oceans;
    the ball became a five by fifteen spread—
    a flat idea projected on a wall.

One day Odysseus crossed to Ithaka;
    then Roland on his mountain blew his horn;
    Dido rose from the ashes of her love;
    Cauchon lit the match that burned up Joan.

Now my long-lived hours recombine the past.
    All time is fiction; in the seas men drown.
    How can I prove my grandfather existed,
    or there's a library where this world will last?

The Side Show Uprising

Like dwarfs they danced on monkey legs
    then juggling tossed their hands aside
The bearded lady shaved off her breasts
    The horses laughed   The little dogs tried

to jump backwards   All the aerialists fell
    On Ararat the ark rested high
and dry   Along the eaves animals
    like gargoyles set across the sky

screamed Stop! as we ran from the theater home
    Praying for what they had nothing of
the homeless died one by one on the cold stones
    unable to bear the grotesques of love

Venus, Half Dressed

Wet and nude like a fish, she lies back;
the curve of her spine sings *Alive, alive-o!*
With the lips of your eyes you kiss her soft hip,
her thigh, her plump calf, each half-painted toe
    like a magnet drawing you into love.

Is this the woman who turned the heads
of old men in Troy? Achilleus's prize
Agamemnon stole? Velasquez's friend
who, in exchange for immortality,
    slept with the artist every night?

Look! A boy has captured her face
in his mirror. There, three figures meet
Time flows like water over soft gray silk.
Space fills with her breasts. In the blue distance
    dawn breaks in the perfect sky.

Three Fish

*The Apostles were so artfully made
that you could take them for living men.*
GOGOL

The fish in Loo Fung Market lie on ice,
    flat their fins and their rice-paper tails.
    Like Madame Defarge at the scaffold, they cast their cold eyes
    on each comer: Who bid you sail
    from the sea into this frozen despair?

Crowned in blue anemones the carp
    laughs with the ladies of its mind.
    The mackerel plucks the seaweed like a harp,
    and the sheepish mullet prays for its lost kind.
    Death is a public pantomime,

last mockery of the carnival of noise.
    Fish, friend, fool—dumb and deaf,
    side by side by the price tags like buoys,
    they wait for whatever action's left,
    as if resurrection were coming next.

Still Life

Behold ten apples on the kitchen table.
        St. Vladimir and a pagan barter on the wall,
        waiting for the samovar to boil.
    (Around the corner the stove now heats the kettle.)
        What do you think: in this otherworldly silence
        should I warn Eve about the devil's apple?

In the Garden of Eden there never was an apple.
        Late one night a scribe inferred a fruit
        to paint the wicked turn the story took.
    (He made the *a* in *malum* a famous letter.)
        Real are the apples of Sodom, which when you touch them
        dissolve in smoke and ashes on the table.

Barnyard

Where wind and water have worked the mortar loose
a gillyflower grows out from the wall,
white-petalled sun of a barnyard solar system:
    spider-comets arcing beneath the crossties,
    midges filtering an azure sky,
a roof, like heaven's dome, all set to fall.

The nervous clouds give away the air.
The birds decline as if in gratitude.
What holds the upright tree against the wind?
    Easy skate down the sidewalk of the modern mind,
    all contradictions melt, the old kinds
of lovers become unisex, and the queen, nude.

Ox tongue, cowslip, purslane — Latin weeds
make salads of Old English words. What stays?
The earth rumbles and rotates all night long
    beneath the animals in the country stars.
    The great wind that sweeps the universe
combles the shards of bare rural days.

Highgate Easter

Snowdrops in the corner of the garden,
      on the earth-filled treads of the cemetery stairs —
white oval bells ringing tempered changes,
      shaking down the soot-rich London air.

High overhead, a hawk; in the ground, bones;
      mortality like vines coiled everywhere —
Old Believers gone, the words lie on the stones:
      No life is true but dying makes it fair.

Time that cycles on the sun around
      row after row of weatherbeaten haloes
sinks in the fish-cold bodies underground —
      down, down like light on a sea of shadows.

Bold men who had to share their cave with bears
      are ghosts along the wall, their carvings glossed
and, like other stones of death, compared:
      Each graven figure is its own cross.

The lambs wait. "Fidem servat." The pocked granite stays
      until the woodbine pulls it down, too.
Then the losers say, *"Je vous baille ma rente de Baugée,"*
      (The wheel has turned; I've nothing to pass on to you).

Men in winter let their language go,
      but the mute earth that stores forsaken goods
bursts in each garden with a mummers' show
      of grace as green leaves overtake the Woods.

On October Ground

Hiking up Mt. Abraham

Honey in the sun-warmed sainted air,
    the cool height where the hawks circle,
    the far blue hills in painted hues,
the last white flowers washed in evening light,
    then the stars floating on a clear cold pool.

Great god of the mountains, unfold the world
    as old Jehovah bedazzled Job.
    Wasn't it you laid the earth's foundations,
set the pillars of Hercules, gave birth
    to the sky, and colored the autumn leaves?

Come, marshal the clouds, scatter the sunlight,
make grass grow on October ground;
    in the immortal night
    give us each other's sound.

Boyd Hill

When I come home to mown field and green air,
    to redcoat maples parading across the sky,
again I hear the music of the soil
    that elsewhere has been poisoned and left to die.

So much depends on death — the city waits,
    enchanted by its weeds, its waste, the time
long gone when Carthage, too, lay flat like a field
    and Dido, in love, heard Aeneas coming home.

April

Soil slips through our fingers; wood smoke
    drifts down the chill wind.
    Minutes are ashen mice
        in the mowing;
      seconds, birds, bones
        on a salver.

On the far hill the firs are blue
    and full against the weather.
    By our stone they point sharp fingers
        to the sky,
      hold heavy clouds
        in place.

Everywhere wild roses, trillium, trout lily,
    a canopy to cover age —
    spring after spring one change
        in sight
      walking day
        and night.

Wild Life

On a Cat Killed by a Pit Bull

The meadow shimmers in the October sun,
    on warm blue asters, like stars fallen from the gravid sky;
by noon the earth, an impatient hunter,
    fires the wind, blacking the trees, searing the fallow.
What can man make with stumps and scorched forms,
    the ridicule of old age, unredeemable failure?

Every false move leads into deeper failure;
    history becomes a dictionary of dead forms,
burned faces on harvested fields lying fallow
    waiting for evil to plow the good under. Then the last hunter
goes cold like the moon, and the silken skirt of the sky
    falls, and wild dogs shred the terrified sun.

Watersong

When I spend a long time fishing alone,
    the brook begins to sing
as if a cemetery of souls in the stones
    were rising in a ring
around me, like a hatch of mayflies,
exulting, then fleeing to the woods.

Why insects are so small is not surprising:
    fact is they have no bones.
What do they make of the moon's rising
    in the firs like an orange stone?
Don't my boots and my two small eyes
trespass on their livelihood?

In our last home we're all alone.
    Some fear forever; some sing.
What's piously carved in the granite stones
    is a joke. Amoral surroundings,
suns swarm and sink in the western skies
without being evil or doing good.

Pistol Star

Intimations of death
Let me wipe it first
Cold-hearted thoughts
sweep the universe
like infrared eyes

find in the dust
graveyards of vastness
galactic lists
the language of nebulae
the landscape of stars

Problems

Simplify
A mind comes apart
so many
tigereyes

Naturals
have secret addresses
knot cutters
no masks

Faces
clouds stories
difficult
the flowers
of grace

Bones in a Landscape

Space is a-fire. The sun burns.
    Rocks melt. Mountains explode.
    I've felt the lust,
    seen the hot lava,
    the kind that caught Pliny
    when Earth's bowels burst.

Two thousand years his bones lay
    unmolested like amber, the Earth circling,
    a necklace strung
    around the sun.
    The snails, the snails!
    Empty, too, the Pleistocene plain.

In the name of the dead the living chose war:
    the rich bought pity from the poor;
    circuses multiplied;
    the zodiac came alive;
    a holy man at the door
    arrested the unfaithful stars.

Conventional

Suppose there were no lines in life:
    no lifelines on a sailing boat,
    no sidewalk cracks, no high tension wires,
    no barricades, no one-way streets,
    no No Man's Land—friend and foe confused,
    not knowing who's to live or die;

how then assemble the body parts
    scattered through Leonardo's *Notebooks?*
    Did the beasts that crowded in the Ark
    have any idea how long it would take
    to reach Ararat? "Soldier on!" they said,
    ignorant of the uniforms of art.

When we come to the Gray Land
    of perpetual twilight where sea and sky
    blur, shadow and substance blend,
    and the moon is as small and cold as the stars;
    when the hard waves have washed our memories away,
    and time, with our lives, has sunk in the sand,

will we think ourselves heaven-bound then?
    Turn over: always the next page is blank;
    the infinite universe balloons
    in the cage of its own unused space,
    like the little pulsing Valentine hearts
        that orbit women and men.

The Grand Illusion

And when he had sat down with them at table, he took bread and said the blessing; he broke the bread, and offered it to them. Then their eyes were opened, and they recognized him; and he vanished from their sight.

LUKE, 24, 30–31; CARAVAGGIO'S "THE SUPPER AT EMMAUS"

for Martha Bates

They're seated at a table; they're about to dine;
there's bread, a well-cooked pheasant, apples, grapes and pears
in a basket, a pitcher, glasses, a flask of wine;
a waiter in a skull cap pays close attention
(closer than a diner gets now anywhere):
it's one of the great works done in 1601 —

like *Hamlet* factual, fancy-free like *Twelfth Night*.
The spirit of change projects the realism.
Why didn't Hamlet have long hair, a light
behind his head, or, like Yeshua, wear loose robes?
Why didn't Polonius forswear provincialism
and like this apostle pilgrimage the globe?

So much is possible. Malvolio thought the best lines
were his, but, emotionally blind like a suicide,
he made himself the corpse of his own paradigm.
He had no idea of Galileo's moons
or that an old man could be astonied
by love in a spiritually crowded room.

Spirit's hands are radiant, as in London
at twilight on a cold December evening
lights from stone buildings strike the smoky clouds
in streaks across a lemon-turquoise sky

and lift the day's mourners out of their grieving.
What the deep faithful see with the mind's eye

is the revelation that the essence of matter, like men,
fills every cathedral and casual eating place.
The born observer who deconstructed the scene
at the height of the drama—one man half out of his chair,
the other with hands flung sideways into space—
painted what was to show what wasn't there.

The bird is untouched; the broken bread is blessed
but uneaten. The waiter's doubt throws the three together.
So masterful is the perspective that you can't guess
what's really there—a cloth-covered table, food,
and figures? or a holy traveller's weather?
or, love found, long loss at last made good?

The Face

How beautiful she was who sang
Wer mich liebt, den lieb' ich wieder,
Und ich weiss, ich bin geliebt
    her face expressing
    what the music felt.

The room was small; the audience, old
lovers as stiff as silver statues
or their own now unremovable rings.
    For one gold moment
    she made their lives sing.

A thousand faces filled the hall
to the music of remembered love
and to the passions their hearts presumed.
    "O poets in your youth,"
    she sang, "bloom, bloom!"

Open and Closed

"The next station is Mornington Crescent. The next station is closed. This train will not be stopping at the next station."
UNDERGROUND ANNOUNCEMENT

How many trains? How many days? Is 'closed'
a solecistic synonym for 'next'?
If 'next' is closed—as unreal as an unread text—

there'll be no stopping, for stopping cannot be supposed
until the train has overtaken itself.
So, reading begins when a book is returned to the shelf.

Count no man happy until he is dead. Who knows
how to measure a life as it goes along?
(That's how Herodotus separates right from wrong.)

In the house of language the halls where the questions are posed
are cold; from the greenhouse off the kitchen, the blooms
of the Red Queen's answers are carried to all the rooms.

Everything means what I say it means. I propose
cutting off *her* head at, say, the station that's next,
which allows you, if you wish, to revise the text

before you've read it. Then on the diagram of rows
of stations, erase what's virtually not there:
in faith, an underground ride is like floating through air.

The Instruction

Poetry from the people, cries the laureate,
    to harvest what the national life has sown,
inviting each reader to tape record a favorite,
    but "the poem you read must not be your own."

The people must have their voices, a poet once declared,
    neither will they bate one jot of ceremony.
Spellbound by the ornate hegemony
    of celebrities and the wealth of the immortal stars,

women pluck lovers from the soap-filled air,
    and men score touchdowns in the beery dark.
Who publishes the writing on the wall?
    Who speaks for the children waiting on the stairs?

After the voices have been had, the tapings played,
    and the people in sober friendliness stand alone,
will they curse the promise they betrayed
    the fact that the poems they read were not their own?

He who scavenged for laurels with a hungry look
    and inked his blood by ripping off the past,
demands that people hold their feelings fast
    and dumbly feed on his (and others') books.

We need not put new matter to his charge
    for there to be justice: time will carve on his stone:
        YOU WHO LIE HERE, NOW READ WHAT LIFE WROTE LARGE,
        BUT THE POEMS YOU READ MUST NOT BE YOUR OWN.

What Are We Waiting For?

Every day
    the cry for justice goes up
        around Columbus Circle
    the curled fists of the homeless
        pummel the sidewalk
    the glass-fingered lawyers
        glide majestically by

Every day
    another promise is broken
        the knees weaken
    another man goes down
        in the store windows
    the mannekins burst into flame
        Lot's wife burns

Every day
    another lie becomes fact
        time washes the streets
    dreams that signify life
        set on West Mountain
    in the stone canyons love
        hovers like plainsong

Every day
    the future shakes free on the fault line
        dividing the present
    thunders into the air
        the mind mushrooms
    It's time it's time What
        are we waiting for

Looking Ahead

The thin mountain air is patient and cool
like a woman's hands that have long made love.
Say the circling hawk is heaven's eye;
say the light is perfumed; the flowers, silk;
    call this the first eternity.

Imagine Elysium unfolding: here come
the asphodel stars. Perseus lives.
The Great Wain drags the universe north—
Polaris, the pulsar, disfiguring time;
    space fulfilling itself like a dream.

Then everything: the future, the past.
Earth's horses canter the Milky Way.
The Pistol Star and the Myth of Er
in tandem gallop around the sun.
    Dark matter seizes the day.

Neither was nor will be, the Great Attractor,
black moon, pangalactic draw,
something from nothing, the secret dies.
Nowhere to go—we breed where we are—
    consumed in natural law.

Circling

Who wants to count the ways in which she's loved?
        Or for that matter, he? Though from desire
        each solemnly deny the proof,
    nine times out of ten the cause of loss is love;
            the source of ashes, fire.

Round and red as an onion, my heart unpeels
        in the November winds. The more that is written,
        the more there is that remains to be said.
    Like ghosts from the past, we set the universe we see
            on the shadows of what's hidden.

A lost world shines in the scarred eyes of the moon.
        Fact: no life without water, no power without blood.
        Olympus was long ago abandoned.
    The wandering souls of the unfaithful cry in the twilight like loons,
            and their feet turn into wood.

Beautiful the rose-striped evening clouds in prayer
        over the blue hills as the pastel sun goes down —
        the woods in dreamy silhouette —
    the constellations, dancing animals in the air —
            a heavenly light coming on.

Flat as a stage, the earth goes round and round;
        the characters dream of being rich and free —
        gold birds in a public garden,
    lovers singing of the future, like Orpheus and
            his lost Eurydice.

Afterword

He learns the pattern of the coming world
who reads the air as like a Persian carpet
     adorned with birds. Monograms blossom
     in the borders. Hunters with lean hounds
   course back and forth across the sky-blue floor.

Upstairs a chorus welcomes each returning hero
and each transubstantiated soul.
     Evil and good ride the sugared breath
     of angels. Wound through the night's immense,
   our language is the burden of our intelligence.